The Eve Of Our Generation

Keanu Joaquin Del Toro

Cover Art by Christian Palacios

Edited and Interior Design by Flor Ana Mireles

Illustrations by Keanu Joaquin Del Toro

1st edition / 01

Paperback ISBN: 978-1-7379393-1-3

Indie Earth Publishing Paperback Edition: December 2021

INDIE EARTH
PUBLISHING

indieearthpublishinghouse@gmail.com

Instagram: @indieearthpublishinghouse

Dear Reader

Bienvenidos, welcome. Enjoy the complimentary coffee on your way in. *Announcement: we're sad to inform you that we've just run out.* This poetry book is divided in a few ways: following the overarching narrative of Jasmine, our main protagonist, through slices of her life; and two sections that have their own little stories, but are wholly unrelated to the mellow and the drama of the Queen of Crayons and Paper Flowers.

One goal I set out to accomplish with this project was to see how far I can blur the lines between prose and poetry, and for the most part, I believe I achieved that — you be the judge. The core of Jasmine's story encompasses Acts I, III and V; I encourage you to follow them like a single watercourse, or to stop and enjoy the many detours between them.

With any of the poems in this collection, I invite you to approach them in whatever way may satisfy you. If you're the type of reader that glances at the last page to get a gauge for the book, you are a lawless soul and welcomed to do so. If you're the type of reader who picks the most intriguing title and works their way from there (very me), be my guest. You choose your own adventure. If you want a love poem, what kind of love are you looking for? If you want something sappy or silly, there's a bit of that, too. Let's get real sad together, and hopefully we won't be too sad for too long.

Table of Contents

I.   Sargasso

The Queen of Crayons and Paper Flowers

When Mami took Jasmine to the store
to help her with the groceries, Jasmine's eyes caught
a glimpse of a box set of sixty-four crayons
and colored pencils. Sixty four of each,
one hundred twenty eight in total.
Colors she didn't even know needed a name
were sitting right before her, a wall dedicated
to rainbows within rainbows within rainbows. She could draw
anything and everything, the groove of wax
shimmering off the page would
be nothing short
of splendid,
brilliant, perfect.
Of course, they weren't
some basic boring bland ordinary Crayola ones
she could find in her own classroom, Jasmine is a more
sophisticated eight-year-old than that. Arteza
is not even a high-end brand, but that didn't matter,
the world — no, the universe was wound up
in the shape of a crayon.
The box set would be creeping close to fifty dollars
plus tax, and Mami wasn't sure if Jasmine was
responsible enough to take good care of it.

But Jasmine simply had to have them, there are more
colors to work with here than there are in a normal twelve pack.
She begged Mami to buy them, and to prove
how much she wanted them
she helped out more around the house, with the dishes,
bathing the dog more frequently, doing things
that were asked of her the first time,
finishing her homework early,
not picking fights with her siblings.

At five,
Jasmine climbed shelves and bed frames
and trees and people if they let her. It's still
the same at eight and nine.
Jazzy, Jaz, Yasmín, ardillita,
bookworm, chipmunk, mapachica,
chiquitita, mi pollita,
she gains a new name for the
little things she does,
the little things
she seems to be.
She brings her questions everywhere
— up the bark of the wrong tree,
down the warrens without a guarantee that
she'll be satisfied with the answers.
For some things, Mami gives her resolution,
but Mami has her work for it,

The answer sleeps in a book or somewhere in a dictionary.

She must invoke it by its name,

break it up with her teeth

and chew it back together
Who put you here?
How long were you waiting for me?

Numbers hiding in a dog's ear,

but she has no such wrinkle in age.

Yesterdays and tomorrows are still so vast,

so endless, out of control, out of reach,
How will we ever get there?

Soon, she will understand that all tomorrows come to her

as easy as they leave.

Mami sighs at her tank top, sprinkle-stained

with bleach from all the cleaning, tossing it in

with the rest of the laundry. She dons

a black oversized graphic tee of Aaliyah and

untangles Jasmine's hair and her own,

now their bronze ringlets smell like coconuts.

Their curls gently clutch the construction paper flowers

Jasmine made in art class, and Mami cups her hands

around a disposable camera from the CVS

around the corner. A grin and a flash.

Ella es siempre la princesita, que queridas mariposas

and all the other little critters that only speak in books

and through the CRT. She dives below the cushions for the remote

to pause the scratched dvd with oily fingerprints, and she draws
what's on screen, and her sisters whine,
it's their favorite scene of *The Little Mermaid*,
but there was no way she'd let it play
without learning how to draw Ariel's tail and feet.
Time crawls frame by glitchy frame, sisters restless and bored,
until Mami reminds her that she's still in her uniform.
Mami rounds them all up for dinner,
Remember to wash your hands before you eat.
Yes, Mami, they comply.
Papi folds his newspaper and
they each clasp their hands and thank Jesus and God
for the food before them, and for another day together,
they pray for their health, and for God to watch over
their family members and their closest friends, amen.

Don't chew with your mouth open, and in the moment they comply.
Don't speak with your mouth full, and in the moment they comply.
You have to say excuse me when someone else is talking.
Don't play with your food.
You have to eat your dinner if you want a surprise.

And Mami does the best she can
for her children to be good and sweet.
Two boxes bundled in gift-wrapping paper
sit on the dining table, and after birthday wishes and song
and ice cream cake lined with ground up chocolate, Jasmine

gives thank you kisses to Mami and Papi,
leaves kisses with their little baby brother eating
his pasty green food and his own
spoonful of cake. The girls scurry off
to their rooms and Jasmine rushes back
to the living room to continue her latest masterpiece,
the wax glowing under the light of the tv.
Papi plucks his little Jasmine off the ground,
a shooting star across a popcorn sky
filled with glow-in-the-dark constellations.

In her years of future nostalgia,
they blocked in her colors between the lines.

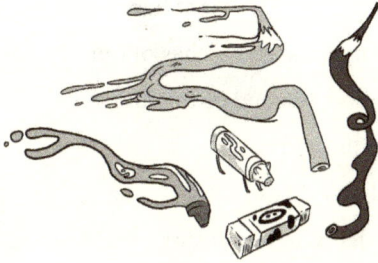

Sailor Sedna

Tiny fingers glide across the blurry ink of
an astronomy book, an atlas of
the heavenly bodies, a single
composite snapshot of the greatest
widest somewhere there is. Jasmine
does not care for the perihelion, there are more
suns burning in the night than there are
sands on a beach, or secrets in the Sahara.

She unfurls a large folded page, the solar system
blooms forth, each planet spinning on a lace
around the sun. With a personal rainbow of
rubber bands on her wrist, Jasmine ponders
how lovely wearing the nine planets like
bracelet charms would be. Her fingers
split into a v, protracting

the distance between planets, from
pole to pole, orbit to orbit. Her right hand
brushes up against the coldest reaches of our
celestial neighborhood, the end of the diagram.
Uranus, Neptune, Pluto, Eris,
Haumea, Makemake, Sedna,
the strange names dance in her mouth.
She is fixated on Sedna.
So remote it's interstellar, searing through
curtains of frost at the edge of everything familiar.
Her d's and n's jut together
pronouncing the name, warring for space
along her alveolar ridge, advancing
to her baby teeth and her permanent ones.
She vibrates the tip of her tongue
with a prolonged th, tickling her teeth
like a bumblebee
trapped in her mouth, a wasp
droning on and on or
a mosquito, fat with blood and sickness.
From her neon pink Jansport bookbag
she slides out a ringed sketchbook
absolutely splattered with stickers, some peeling
and fuzzy with lint. There are so many
stickers of puppies and starfish
and dolphins and flowers and pizza

and smiley faces and crescent moons and
kittens and onomatopoeia
that the sketchbook's true cover
cannot be seen beneath the foliage
of utter kawaii. She shakes out her
color pencils from their box and
scratches out some blue and yellow,
then, purple, red, and even more purple,
until the flurries of waxy wonder and
whimsy coalesce into her best drawing yet.
Sailor Sedna, her own OC, who has recently
awakened as the newest Sailor Guardian, as
the description on the corner of the page narrates
in this nine-year-old's best handwriting.

Sailor Sedna could touch the stars, in a blink
she's there, wherever she wants to go, she's there.
Nothing is too distant, no lightyear too vast,
only a stretch in time. Jasmine has only
ever known the endless heat of Miami, Florida's
perpetual monsoon season that feels like it really
ever stops for just a handful of weeks, only to return
not with a vengeance, but a warning, a reminder,
a guarantee of devastation.
She has only ever known hurricanes.
She'd pray for snowstorms to cancel school instead,
those sound much more fun.

January

Middle child, between Jasmine and Jupiter.
Peacekeeper, it's safer
to follow the tried and tested truths
than question their validity. Cozy is burritoed in a blanket
with hot cocoa before bed, cozy is jackets
and oversized hoodies even when it's hot outside,
cozy is nobody has to fight.
Dressed for function and comfort, not to
stand out like Jaz, not to fit in like Jupe.
Each an attention seeker in their own respect, but Jan
can blend in with the rest of the pedestrians, cool
as cucumber slices sitting in a glass of water, her voice
as satisfying as the crunch.

Keanu Joaquin Del Toro

Niñez sabe a Chícharo

Toda la familia sleeps with a full stomach
with a bowl full of chícharo.
When she's split like a pea, or
sick and cozy, pobrecita pachuchita,
little Jasmine flower.

When summers are scarce and the weather's fragile,
chícharo, steaming or chilly, is so ideal.
See how the chicken peels off the bone so well,
grains of rice snuggled in a warm green blanket,
o cómetelo como una sopita, qué chachi, qué chévere
chícharo!

Rose-Tinted Glasses from the Dollar Store

if you never wanted to play outside
if none of your days were ever tie dyed
if none of your friends
had ever seen you cry
you didn't have a childhood

if you never bit the heads off your animal crackers
if you never solved the riddles on the back of all the wrappers
if you never pretended
your hands were toy clappers
you didn't have a childhood

never faked being sick so you can stay home from school
never got all pruny, made it warm in the pool
if you never at least once
broke every single rule

if you never stayed up late to watch [as] after ten
never wanted to become a teen or a titan
if you never skipped
while holding hands with friends

never had your first kiss before senior high
never had a failing grade or two to hide
if you never wanted
to get away with lies

if you never caught a storm that was raining cats and buckets
never had a day without a couple of fuck its
if you always had some ketchup
to dunk your chicken nuggets

if your hand-me-downs never made it past you
if mosquitoes never bit or you never had a zit
if you never misplaced
a single pair of shoes

if you never got lost for just a couple hours
never sat in trees just to catch the breeze
if you never made believe
you had latent superpowers
you never had a childhood

if you never felt alone on Christmas
or hollow in October
or hungry giving thanks
or never ate the leftovers
if you were never on a litmus
or pushed to your limits
you never had a childhood

at least not mine

Jupiter

hyperactive little shit who knows she's adorable.
limelight, lemondark
caution giving sugar, she can be a bit sour.
tiniest of the trio, but she still wears rings.

she's babysitting you, not the other way around.
rose water, cinnamon-'nemone, lavender ice cream,
loudest in the room, technicolor chunky shoes,
bumpin' pandora radio licking off the icing of an oreo
mint chocolate hating, cookie jar breaking,
pokemon the first movie soundtrack kinda girl,

but she's sweet once you get to know her.

A Sleepover with Social Learning at the Tender Age of Ten

Phoebe shifts in her sleeping bag,
huddled in the hush after dark.

"Jaz, are you awake?"

"No," she yawns. "Are you?"

"I've gotta tell you something… I'm bi."

"Bi?" Jaz sits up. "Where are you going?"

Sargasso Sea

Thanksgiving was the last time they played house.

Ginebra and her daughters had a picnic spot
near the bridges and the highway. In her
early-mid twenties, few spaces across urban
society don't expect you to spend money, beaches
and libraries each an oasis endangered. This
has only exacerbated throughout Jasmine's childhood.
Autumn underwater, not as pretty, just as delicate.
Along the shore, carpets of algae a dull briny brown.
Blunt and brunt, the awkward swirling about the
intertidal zones with no place to rest. At home, aimless
talk, abbreviated.

The beach is sanctuary, solitude, where

Ginebra — and Jasmine after her — feel
natural, native. The clutter and tangle of
family trouble set to soak, drama among
peers and friends on pause, stress over school
exfoliated. She can scatter it far enough to
ebb and silhouette into the blue beyond her.
She doesn't have to keep face here.
Mami would say, "Look, when you sift
through the sargazo, you can find little
shrimp and crabs and even caballitos hiding."

Her tips dipped in gold, the blonde stream had
trickled down rusty drain, the tub gurgled
and coughed up the chemicals. Dyeing her hair
was a very heated topic, Jasmine would seethe,
independence radiating, her mother shut off the
stove, dismissive. When she finally did it, though,
there was little fight in either of them.
Only tension.

The palms and banyans mitigate
with the wind. Broad in leaf, under
their shade her sweat is relief
and not a "slick nuisance," as her teacher
once called her. The seaweed, dark
as her roots, tender and slippery
under her soles. She marches till

she's buoyant, the sun retreats

behind clouds, proud in their conquest.

Knowing she's too close to shore for the

shelf to drop, she anticipates, expects

the abyss to be dismal, remote,

capricious as it is cold. Teeming around

hydrothermal vents, life knows day

without sun, thriving

under all that pressure.

Suppress the buildup, a sudden island.

## II.	Under the Canopy of My Family Tree

Somewhere in Cuba (I Hope You Find Peace)

Frugal, brutal, forever frustrated

shade is welcome but not when you trade blows with it

heated words are flammable

they cast long shadows

don't confuse my passion for being rude and offensive

not every conversation switches who's on the defensive, this

 is not a battle, it's breakfast, it's dinner

yet you blow your warhorn, wartorn, battleworn

is this the world you were born in?

is it the santos, your ghosts or your skeletons?

friendly fire, first blood, the world a black and white

environment — at some point bearing arms is no longer a

requirement. your nature meets your nurture, volatile,

combative, passive and active aggressive anger

seamless with regret cause you're skilled with your hands

your plans, why was your art never part of it?

buckets, barrels, bottles, jars full of cowrie shells and beads

the need to save them all.

Keanu Joaquin Del Toro

Cookie tins full of yarn is expected from abuelas

but magazines for old telenovelas

gum wrappers, old tissues, moldy clothes, stacks of newspapers

five different nail clippers, one looped with your keys

knick knacks and angelitos, gowns with permanent creases

magnets without a fridge, board game pieces paired

with chairs and recliners and dilapidated sofas

all competing for attention in a tiny space

hoping that one day someone relays

they really need child-sized dolls that blinked in the most

unnerving way imaginable, they're all just too sentimental

dozens of boxes, every cosita un tesoro

on moving days, you work me like un toro

sewing kits and threads for clothes you rarely made

blades that slaughtered chickens and goats

dulled from rust and old age, scissors to meet the edge now

there's nothing left to selvage — you're selfish

except when you're not but that's just guilt

— it's woven in.

Good graces were reserved only for guests and strangers

con familia, it's, "¡Respetame!"

stitched into every fight, demanded like it's tribute

but we'd never need a rearview to see the real you.

it's not like I doubt your love

you just had your own way of showing it

spoiling us by breaking bread with pizza

videogames and ice cream

and shouting matches and miércoles and mentiras

reminders of where these nice things came from

just to stay relevant

I know it hurt your pocket and the gestures were nice but we

always had a reason to feel guilty

and for all the time I've known you and your bony hands

you eat, sleep, drive and clean in torment

some part of you left dormant and

screaming and crying

somewhere in Cuba.

Keanu Joaquin Del Toro

You're a living mystery

history begins before you, but only finds shape with Mami

and some days that can sit bitter

I learned to accept it

but the practice of living mysteries dies with you

your siblings, and mostly with you

because I know myself, Mami knows herself

because I am Miami, Cuba, Puerto Rico

I am a citizen of the world —

I know this has little to do with me

and more to do with your parents

your loss and grief and the trauma they inflicted

especially with your mother

and how you didn't get to say goodbye

how it all feeds into self destructive tendencies

because you either don't know better

or don't want to know better

and that you don't know how to articulate any of this

and on some level

that's just how it is

this is not grace or forgiveness

it's understanding.

Abuela,

I hope you find peace.

Bendición.

Amen.

Philadelphia

pollitos and french fries were his first words

his peanut butter fingers clutch a toasted pb and j

after school tequeños in the microwave

trapped in beats cooked in vaporwave

bahama bucks pro skater

tropical smoothie soothsayer

wannabe somewhere else but stuck at home

porky

he's too teenage for most books

he's too smug for most girls

too young to rule the world

too old to whine about everything else

like the other kids with his pumped up kicks

decked out in multi-colored threads for military balls

as decorated as a high schooler can get

he stays up all fortnite

and marches playing soldier

i hope he's ready to be a real one

eighteen coming fast

and taking forever to get dressed

he walks over homework, straight for arizona

while his mind tramples into his ever longer body

he's cocky he'll be taller, but for now

he's still shorter

waiting restless for his life-to-go order

from this side where the moon climbs

he's still my baby brother

no matter how much the sun burns his ears

no matter how much his antics stretch mom's face

no matter how much he wrinkles his math homework

no matter how much I wanna smother him, home is always

philadelphia

—*Echolalia*—

"Buba, use your words. 'I want.'"

"I want."

"No, you say it, papi."

"Please."

"You have to say it together. 'I want…'"

"Please."

"Say, 'I want Ipad please.'"

"Please."

"Buba… what do you want?"

"Ipad, please."

"Good job!"

I give him the iPad, "What do you say?"

"Thank you, you're welcome," he spits out.

I understand why you get frustrated,

or at least part of it.

Sometimes I'm contradictory,

inconsistent. Sometimes I'm too loud

or I get to be when you don't, we

turn up our music when we get down,

you crank up the theme songs

for Danny Phantom on loop and Luigi's Mansion in rotation

why can't the rest of the house hear it?

You may feel left out,

left behind, it's hard

to even physically arrange the question

why

because the answer

may not be satisfying, may not be

what you were really looking for

when you were always looking for me

or us

or someone else

who's always somewhere else.

I understand.

That I understand.

It's okay to feel this angry, this flustered,

this aggravated, because here you are heard,

here you are acknowledged. The feeling

passes, I don't see you wear it

when I'm here and now and present —

you are stronger when you smile, when you laugh.

I see the you that others choose to overlook

and that's their loss

because you are my Buba

you are always here with me and I am here with you.

Your Son

It's been hard being away, we both know that. It's been hard
being away.
I remember a conversation we had, it's one we tend to
cycle through every now and then.
Part of it goes like "So you believe in nothing?"
"No, I don't believe in nothing, I'm not a nihilist."
"Then what are you? What do you believe?"

I believe in you, in what you're capable of. In every degree,
even if I've yet to agree, I believe you make the right choices,
because they're usually the hard ones.
I believe that burning sage helps mellow us out because it
mellows you out.
I believe you're as real and as deep as life and love get,
the whole of you
a body of water a thousand men like me and a million more
could drown in.
I believe in kindness, because you showed me what it was, led
me to the water when I wouldn't drink, you gave me
providence
like no god could. You taught me the hymns that die
unspoken, and hymns for smaller fish others won't catch.
I believe that heaven is the way the living room is rearranged
every season.

I finally believe in me, for a long time I didn't.

When I looked at you then, I believed I couldn't be happier.

When I look at you now, I'm just as stunned by how time

found us here so soon.

God may give you strength when you need it, and despite that,

I give all the credit to you.

I believe that God cannot

and can never

love you the way I do.

Love,

— Your Son

Pretending to be Bilingual

I didn't know you,
any of you. Not even
when I really wanted to.

For you, Forefather, bearer of my name,
it was all the same with your own son,
my old man.

And like your son,
my old man,
what I knew was an aquifer,
histories essentially permissible
to dissipate instead of permeate
through me. There was never
much to drink at these wells
because once words were exchanged,
they ran dry, our words would evaporate
and whatever secondhand news or
sources sprung up would
pool together to commiserate
each and every one of you.
A pity. Such a pity that
while I've lived in the same city with three of you
I really only knew one, only struggled with one
to sift through my broken spanish and her english,
long rusted over, I have only had to pretend

to be bilingual every day with just one of you.

I do not condemn either of you, it's just a pity.

It's not even too late for three of you, it's just defeating.

I am as much a stranger to each of you

as you are to me, so why stress on a limited vocabulary?

Latin-X-Latino

i'm reclaiming what i gave up long ago

my tongue

my heritage

my faith

my eyes are not the first thing other eyes meet

my smile is not the second thing other smiles greet

it goes my skin, my hair, my eyes and my smile

or my hair, my skin, my smile, my eyes

these are just some of my inseparable me-nesses

that i no longer hide or keep to myself

i was taught shame for having hair like a jew

i was taught shame for having skin like a muslim

my skin was too dark to hang out with some white kids

my skin was too light to keep up with some black kids

my name was unusual, i was persian to someone, kenyan to

another, hawaiian to someone, lebanese to another, i was

italian to someone, mexican to another

i wasn't cuban enough, not boricua enough

not white enough, not black enough, not honduran enough,

not a taurus enough

i was taught shame for speaking spanish

i was taught shame for not speaking enough of it

my tongue was a fire that i put out too quick

— At Nowhere's Heels in Semantic Drift —

when i was a guppy in a sea of puberty
at fourteen, i opened my heart to you
the wittiest, funniest girl i ever knew
so eager to mythologize solidarity

at fifteen i lifted you and buckled beneath our weight
we shattered in disparate rain pools
a sister in spirit, and under rapid spate
you went dancing, romanticizing your ghouls

hands traded for acceptance, both in short supply
resolve surrendered to abuse
out the corners of your world, and to its depths applied
at sixteen you wept, *what's the use?*

fallen stars are faulty, unheard wishes and cries
your eyes, your hair in rotation,
with another's expectation,
the yesterdays streamed out, bleeding out with the dyes

it's hardest to be satisfied by open-ended goodbyes
plain to see that we leave them out of view
yet it's painful to watch you strain yourself so small
squeeze into what someone else decides
is right for you —
when do you decide
what's right for you?

twenty-two candles and a hurricane — it's no contest
what ails, what weathers, chips, and peels
with every passing word, even i have to attest
we find our way at nowhere's heels

despite all the love i showed you i could shoulder
my warmest hugs only left you colder
i realized too late it had little to do with me
yet i chose to take it personally

sailing through the doldrums with a passive voice
whenever the stars peek through the light noise
it's hard to make out where they've been
i've made a lot of mistakes, now and then

i wasn't leaving you behind
you didn't want to follow me
i tell myself it was justified
the river fell and arose the litany

the grammar of waterwheels
obsolesced with our new slang
and what once had text appeal
played in empty rooms, no one heard it sing

like one of those fireflies lilting in the night
redshifting from drinking age to twenty five
two earthly bodies lost in semantic drift
i'm no longer what i was before the rift

my consonants fizzle out, evaporate

the silt our personal sahara

it's been a long time since we were twenty-two

when do you decide?

i hope you did

i hope you do

Keanu Joaquin Del Toro

BLOOD

What is blood
 if it's too thin to move through the body,
gravity working against it, the wilt in your leaves,
meat peeling off the bone of the cage full of heartache?
What is blood
if it's too diluted, too distilled, too macerated
in twenty thirty forty plus years of apathy — disillusion —
disgust?
What is blood
if it's too low in iron,
an element stable enough to hold this planet together?
What is blood
if it's too weak to donate to your brothers
since you refuse to be the lifeline?

You can't see how you shoulder the same
childhood fears and traumas,
so you'd rather harp on, replay, rewind, burn and scratch
the same adulthood melodramas that ferment
boiling in the salty stink of your collective shit upbringings.
When your joints stiffen from the weather —
when your bad knees that kept you from going pro
lock and shut you out from your ethnic background noise —
let the shittiness wash over you —
some germs are good for you —

water your grass instead of hosing it down with your
thumb over the spout to quicken the process because you're
just too impatient and have better things to do.
You still have time slated to feel sorry for yourself
after you catch the game.

Instead of boxing up the memory
or the name that shocked you like a
doorknob to the room your hurt breeds behind —
chained like a pitbull for the cock-fight,
zipped up for the dick-measuring contest,
duffled in leather, the plastic dreams,
the lifestyles that choke your wildlife with
domesticated violence and child abuse —
ask yourself
why your nerves are shot every damn time.

What is blood
when it's forsaken from the body based on association
with the life you're not satisfied with
while you hide behind pictures online?
Oh, the boys are amazing, in fact they're doing fine?
They're all getting married and leaving you behind?
Or are they off living their own lives and leaving you the fuck
out?
Mom is doing great, thanks for asking. The boys are fantastic,
oh

you know? about my baby brother and his high school pics of
him
in his camo as he staffs the red white and blue?
The pics of him in his beret with the ribbons he earned
and the grin you could never slap off his face,
but you didn't reach out, did you?
He had to send the first text, huh?
Did you ever think that'd be a great way to bond, reconnect or
did you already forget you were military men, too?
All of you were soldiers, but I see no honor in that.
I see no Pursuit of Happiness in either of you,
I see no acquisition of the American Dream.
But I see it in my baby brother,
my little Porky,
my pollitos and french fries with Arizona on the side.

What is love for your neighbors, your friends, for strangers
and others
When you lack love for your mother, your father, your sisters
and brothers?
Do I expect you to be perfect?
No, man, but I expect you to be real.
Don't bullshit me, what reason do you have to bullshit me
when all these years later I'm reaching out to you
because I want to piece your sorry ass past together and make
sense of you?
Or is that where I'm going wrong?

Do I expect too much of you?
Don't be a mouthpiece for someone else to blow hot air out of,
Don't speak from both ends of your mouth,
Don't be conniving and work my mother
into the sob story that obviously left you with bruises and scars
way before my mom got stitches from her first three times in
delivery rooms.
Don't start a dialect,
start a dialogue.

You still wanna play twenty questions? I've got twenty more:
Could you, as brothers, hug each other?
 Kiss them on the forehead or the cheek?
Could you wear each other's handmedowns instead of fucking
them or complaining?
Could you slip into sleep in the same part of town,
on the same street, under the same roof, in the same room,
in the same bed, sharing the same sheets as your brothers?
Could you listen to each other's problems instead of
blaming them and others for all of yours, instead of
bringing up old shit? Could you actually remember
each other's birthdays instead of
the he-said-she-said fifteen years ago?
Doesn't that bother you?

Doesn't it bother you
that I look so much like you?

That you look so much like your brothers?

That you never came around because you didn't want a

retarded son or daughter?

"Oh, sometimes people get so caught up being angry for so

long

that they forget what they were angry about."

Are you sure you're not talking about you?

It's called projection —

this is the same image you keep showing the class like it's

gonna be on the test.

"Caught up being angry" — why are you heated?

what war are you fighting?

What victory are you dying for?

What promised land are you crossed you couldn't find?

What paradise was lost? What is your tribe?

What do you bequeath to your sons when you die?

Do the sins of the father visit the sons

or are they permanent members of the household?

What legacy do I see when you pass the torch,

or are you busy burning forests

when you meant to burn the bridges?

Do I expect you to be perfect?

No.

You're not my martyr,

so stop nailing yourself to crosses

when we speak about the past

you want to leave behind in tail-lights,

and yet you're always the

helpless defenseless five-foot-ten 200-pound epicenter

of muscle mass and pity in your narrative.

What happened?

Old man, I know why my father up and left,

sperm-banks like to do that when they cash out before

child support fucks them in the ass.

But what about you?

At the very least, tell me why you weren't around.

"I don't know what went down. That's not my place."

Those don't mean the same thing.

I only want to know your side of things

there are a lot of gaps in my life about you

for all of you.

"If I tell you the truth, and you feel a certain type of way, that's

on you."

That applies to you, too. What are you getting defensive for?

maybe you were shot a long time ago, messenger

but I didn't pull the trigger.

"I don't wanna say anything bad about your mother."

"I don't wanna get derogatory."

Why do we even have to take it there?

We're talking about me and you.

If you felt "a certain type of way"

Did you ever tell her how you felt, how you feel?

"Your mother is not the kind of person you can reason with."
Of course not. You didn't even try.
Cause when I spewed bullshit, I got my ass beat by her, too,
The difference is I can reason with her.
I grew patient — we allowed ourselves to.
She's got a Master's degree in Psychology —
but you didn't know that —
you siked yourself out of being present in our lives —
you stopped asking and reaching out to me
before and after my puberty.
And what the actual fuck does your beef with my mom have to
do with me?
She's vegan, you fucking assholes.

I know it doesn't look like it, but I used to be angry.
Once upon a time I expected more from the men
I grew up believing were the strongest men in the world —
not these sorry ass excuses who believed they're owed
forgiveness.
What is blood when you choose money —
when you choose yourself —
every —
single —
time?
Isn't that the same shit you're pissed at your parents for?
The safest place in my world is falling asleep on the couch

with my mother and my brothers at my side.
One of the best things I've got to look forward to
is that I will grow old and ugly and grey
and still never turn out like any of you.
I'm not angry,
I'm disappointed
because my elders would rather make their own kin blind
than allow them to see themselves for who they really are
and yet you all show it without even knowing it.
you can fall of the grid or slip right through it
start over in a new city, a new corner of the globe
but you are always a resident in your state of mind
it's the loneliest kind — it's the worst prison
the world won't slow down to hear you when
there's so little left to say
maybe that's what happens when the grudge is too deep
— the kids are the common casualty

Little Big Sister

I am my older sister's big brother,
one of her many binge buddies
and her private modern renaissance artist
when she desires a new commission —
for the last year, the theme has been
consistent mashups of My Little Pony with
all her favorite media. Just dozens of late-2000s style
amv-esque crossover fanart that defined millennials
like us. I'm her big brother because I can feed her
and the rest of the family, I can lace her shoes
and know when it's not too tight, I can give
piggyback rides, pick her up when she falls
and catch her before she does, I pick her and
Buba up from school, and I always find her tv

remotes and her movies when she loses them.
As soon as I started making money,
I, too, contributed to Kassy's personal movie library fund,
our own Disney vault before there was a plus at the end,
and even then, she is not satisfied. She will
never be content, because it's the content
that matters to her, not the quantity. Her own
qualitative measurement for how fixated
she is with her latest obsession is directly
correlated by how much she talks about it,
how many drawings she requests, how many
pictures from Google images she wants to print out.

When she doesn't want to write something down,
she tells me that her hands are too big, it's her way
of saying that she has a hard time holding a pen or
marker, that her hands, her tiny thin delicate hands
shake so much that she's self-conscious about them.
So we practice often, it's easy to motivate her when
she writes the title of a movie she likes, or writes
all our names, our phone numbers, where we live,
how old she is, her favorite food, *keep it simple,*
sweetheart. We jam in space together,
we count down birthdays and every holiday
and mark our calendars when a movie's
coming soon — yes, it's coming soon —
on most days, it's simple and clean.

Quarantine was hard on everyone, and it was
very trying on Buba and Kassy, they went from
going on field trips with their school every week
to staying home indefinitely. We had to remind her
and Buba to keep it safe, that we have to wear our
masks and wash our hands, cover our mouths when
we cough and sneeze (they remember that most of the time),
that Target is closed because people are sick
so we can't go to the dvd aisle on a movie run
like we used to. She prayed for her friends
from school, did her best to behave and be a
good girl, and we were understanding when
she felt cooped up and didn't tell us directly,
because we all felt like shut-ins and hermits eventually.
But we kept our sanity and most importantly, our peace.
We went to the park a lot, walked around the neighborhood
in the evening, ate dinner and watched movies
in the backyard (can you guess her favorite word?)
We are a family that is very big on cinema.
We're all visual learners here, and all of us sitting
with Kassy and Buba through The Polar Express
while drinking hot cocoa, or only catching the first ten
 seconds of the Danny Phantom theme song,
starting Gilmore Girls all over again,
getting hyped for an Avengers marathon,
watching anything with them is important, integral

to our connection with them because
when we're an audience together, we show them
that they matter, their interests matter, that we care.

Kassy and Buba always need a little help,
they take care of us just as much
as we take care of them, in ways they
don't grasp, but they feel.
I really believe they do.
Kassy and Buba taught us so many lessons
on humility, appreciation for the company of others,
how to look after each other,
what it means to be there for someone who
deserves it. We always need a little help, and it
doesn't take much, just a bit of earnest,
a smile, a hug, something that says *I see you,*

you are alive,

and you are worthy of love.

"Wasteland"

Blue Period

habitual leftovers for breakfast

three after noon

laundry heaped in basket, never folded.

cups and bottles and cans and candles

in vigil to muffled curse, witness to vague

hushed sobs and weeping so as to not wake anyone up.

jamie drinks galaxies

cold against the charms on her anklet

learning chord progressions by paramour

crushing on girls in red.

time slows down when it knows

it's being watched

it's why the best way to kill it

is to forget it's there.

it's mistaken to be the same with people

and the things they won't let go;

neglect, ignorance

to forget

lets it all seem like it was

never even there, but what stays is regret.

how do you accept what's going well

when you don't acknowledge what went so wrong?

where the fuck do you even begin?

Going to the Wizarding World Just to Try Some Butterbeer

Yeah, she's a know-it-all
because she had to know enough
to get by, to be seen, to be heard.
It wasn't enough to be smart.
She has to be witty, spontaneous,
but organized, rehearsed in
the steps to be dependable, reliable
in it for herself, but not selfish.
Hungry, but not starved. Coy, coquettish
tapping it, but not thirsty, opportunistic
not parasitic, symbiotic not
one-sided, nobody's deadweight,
first place in her weight class.
Know-it-alls make it obvious
because it is to them.
The What If episode with Latina Hermione
when the memory of her parents wasn't worth erasing,
when she was worth preserving
remembering.

In-tarot-gating the Future

Strength reversed, Ace of Pentacles upright.

Ace of Cups not upright, not reversed, it fell off the table

and landed sideways, the dining room light

dull on her anklet charms.

Aquarius and the Pleiades, a centaur and the north star

flat across canyons in the wood,

the little ants that proceed and die without her, or you

or any of us,

Invisible until they make themselves known.

Muisje

Anne radicalized her.
She slipped into the sleeves of Kitty so snug, so well.
Anne just wanted to be herself, yet she hid in fear,
fear of what others would say and do to her. It was
life and death. She was starving for love and
acceptance, to be liberated not only from the mausoleum,
but from the confines of her age, her own time.

She wept every night for weeks, endless dreaming
of fire, an eternal slice of silence.

Blinking One Too Many Times

If matter cannot be
created nor destroyed
then maybe
I was always here, just not
here in one place
in one human collective or animal
sharing the same breathing
room or eating fatty foods
and abrasively washing my
face until I get the blackheads
out. If so, you were always
here, too, just somewhere else
someone or thing or two else
for epochs
eons
geological time scales
interstellar lifetimes
so it should not hurt so damn much
being without you.
For most of my life
I lived without you
so don't hit me up
after the sun left town
to interrupt my laying in bed braless
in mosquito net summer

while I shuffle and skip what's

on my repeat.

I don't wanna know where you are

I don't wanna dream of *whatcouldhavebeens*

I don't need some body

not always.

medusa and the male gaze

unwanted attention.
    mundane bodies in her orbit.
    self revised? reimagined? recontextualized?
    self-consciousness.

eventually,
    a girl is meant to hide from the world
    — self-loathing an adopted mantra. a part of her
    does not, cannot, belong. the sacred
    is soon profane — both are not meant to touch, but
    are nonetheless deserving of privacy, of space
    to exist. a girl is meant to take up space
    yet she is shy anyway — uncomfortable,
    reserved, cautious, wary, fearful, embarrassed
    to be a girl. this is all taught.
    defiance attracts discipline, etiquette
    is a shoe that's broken in,
    something tends to break.

when she is still underage,
    she receives lecherous, lascivious
    lashes against the skin, sin
    immediate, crystallized, blemished. distant smirks
    and glances, passing advances committing her body
    to memory. so easy are those eyes to gouge,
    but it does little to blind them all.

the eyes behold what they will,

their gaze clings on to the mere scarcity of skin,

the eyes crave what races the blood — what is

hidden brings surprise, expectation, a demand

to be known, not necessarily understood.

is there holiness in ignorance?

is their villainy in apathy?

the words curl around her lips and through her teeth,

> *it's not my fault i'm beautiful,*
> *but it's yours for reminding me.*

but

> *it's my fault*

is what skips and repeats.

the curvature of her disdain,

these curls are not for foreign

fingers to loop around,

yet they do without asking.

permission denied by her killer glowers

and acid rain. must the mountain

concede to a passive plain?

how a girl brings the room, the atmosphere

to a halt, to falter

when she declares

a kinetic,

electric

No.

few things in the world

bring righteous wicked anger

like that simple word.

few things petrify and fossilize irreverence.

if nothing was sacred, then all things are —

if all, then none. the value of things

is confused to revolve around its use,

bound by commodity and comparison.

is someone sacred, someone worthy

of love and respect

if she has to convince you? to barter

for her freedoms, her body, her soul,

her vagina, her silent soliloquies,

monologues on mute?

sacred is she

who fights to be worthy.

sacred is she

who knows she already is.

sacred is she

who has yet to know this. dignity

a pang in the throat, unreleased

when people-pleasing others

— beauty not for beauty's sake,
but for her own. in this,
in one breath, one syllable:
the ultimate source of power. there is
something to stand up for, something
to deny. the sacred is not granted, it is
earned and respected, reciprocal,
not one-sided.
first, she must respect herself.

pride is not the antithesis of shame,
but it's source. she was taught the
language of shame, she must pick up
the words from another dialect
before she speaks in tongues. it will be as
strange and unconvincing as an accent, yet
to reevaluate her inner dialogue she has to
listen to what she's telling herself,
sift through her personal narratives
and whose word is spread — is she
preaching her own truths, or is she chanting
gospel someone else shamed into her?
in nature, you find what you nurture,
what you nurture becomes your nature —
when you pit ego against id
you are not at peace.

she is full of mistakes, and once she accepts that
    she can appreciate her small victories
    and achieve the big ones. she can — she has the strength
    and the power to. it comes with belief. she can
    obey mami and papi, she can run it by her friends,
    she can take every grain of salt and season with it,
    and it will mean little if she declines to become
    the woman she knows she is.

She is haiku

As obsidian,

flaky, prone to spark and light,

dormant till release.

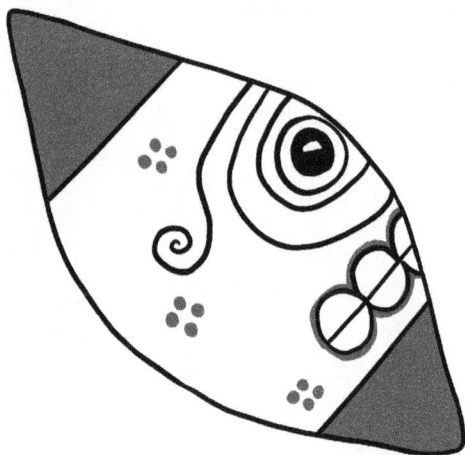

La Cueva de las Manos

ochre red and charcoal black,
writing and wisdom,
wordless, yet teeming with history, personality
at the place of duality,
beyond river and hill,
waving hello from a safe place or
doing their best to say goodbye.
like branches of a bush, a great tree fanning out,
enough shade to catch the sun,
or anemone undulating far below —
they float in this middle ground
between now and then, sea and sky.
a collage of utter humanity, or blowing wishes
like cinnamon on sandstone to
the hunter's moon, or celebrating
something, a memo stating, *we were here,*
hiding in the safety of the earth.

we are fractals, a series of spirals, it's evident —
your individual human spirit meanders
down the lifelines creased, splintered
like the cold stare of europa
with you everywhere you go, inalienable.
ripples billow out, stationary, lifetime forever,
natural geography of the human body.

dactylograms, fingerprints
are one of the many ways
the body conveys we are who we are.
our bones remember our diet long after
we forget hunger, they work around the fractures
and make it clear how much stress we were under,
the weight we carried with us.
what will you be remembered for,
how will others know you were here?
by the metric tons of plastic you used up,
the change in your coastline
or how good you make someone feel today?
start small, you have galaxies grooved
and etched into your palms.

Moving Away, Not Quite Moving On

She doesn't look for trouble, trouble
finds her. She's minding her own
damn business with her nose in a
book before Suzy or Sasha or Cristina
or Helena or Hippolyta or Jake or Benicio
or whoever the fuck rope her into high school
melodrama. Beyond tired, she's bored
of being the mediator between everyone's bullshit.
Folding the legs of her jade tinted shades, she asks,

      "Why can't you guys just figure it out
yourselves? I've got way too much homework
to do and I don't see any of y'all mofos
doing it for me."

      JUST LEAVE ME THE FUCK ALONE.
      I CAN'T WAIT TO LEAVE THIS CITY.

    …but she could wait, she was never okay
        with open-ended goodbyes.
   "See you when i see you," feels so cold,
unaffectionate, despite being on and off with
  receiving hugs. Today, she welcomed them.
    The gradual incline rattled the car
      making it feel its age, air tucked
too deep in her ear and wouldn't leave her be
  like an unwanted stranger that couldn't

get a clue to gracefully fuck off right now.

New town, new school, new everything.
Not a taste of independence, meal after meal of it.
She does aight.
Her grades have rarely if ever been the issue before,
now she's really going through the shit.
Despite how much they annoyed her
and how many fights they had,
Jaz really missed Jupe and Jan. They were divine
compared to her roommates
and suitemates, who lived filthy,
fought dirty, fucked loud
and used all of the toilet paper and tampons.
She still had fun, sure, but
("Not everything is rendered void by the use of but,"
Jaz loves to argue)
she's yet to find her clan, find her footing.
Big personalities behind every door down every hall.
Even at a state school, what the hell does she have to offer?

IV. Liminals

The Boy Who Cried

I was a boy who cried

often, too much

rarely, not enough

as a baby, a toddler, a little nothing

when someone looked at me and

I didn't like their face

I poured, and snot ran down my chin every

now and then, I

make the smallest flinch when

someone looks at me with

anger, contempt, a deep scarred sadness

in my twiggy tweens and small time adolescence I'd cry when

I was frustrated when

my words wouldn't come out when

I got in trouble when

I was a wall when I

felt alone I am

now a man who cries every now

and then the best cry is the

snot-flowing kind, the

headaching goosepimpled shivering cold sitting

in the shower lying on the

tile good heavy cry

I love the release, the head rush when

my mind and my body sync back together when

the world feels a little crisper

a little more raw when

my mother cries when

my siblings weep when

I offer my friends my shoulder when

I click my heels because there's no place like home when

kittens and puppies yelp and mew when

I mourn the days of my wasted youth when

I'm high-strung and forever young when

leaves from the vine are falling so slow when

my little soldier boy comes marching home

I cry even harder then because it's so real

and I love the release

Open Letter from a Racially Ambiguous American

how does a bastard

becomes the master of his life —

strain the pain from the strife

when he's stricken with fear —

goosebumps like spring chicken?

it quickens the blood

sits in the mud, sickens and shudders

the seat of his emotions he stutters

what's on his mind from the storm leaving his insides

worn out, torn out, born out of more

frustration to pin down on the chopping board

the memories he hoards for rain every day

soaked and musty, iron will turned rusty

lips and nails gone crusty

you can bring a horse to water

but you can't make him drink

yet he's parched and breaks apart

with every parting till he sinks

how does a bastard

follow the herd as he speaks without a word?

if you're feeling analytical, let's get political —

when was the last you heard of youth empowered

to march during a global pandemic?

critical race is the only epidemic

I'mma catch a cold with

because I pursue education

I'm naturally broke

I'm not broken, I'm outspoken

no token for your trope

I'm no statistic, not a mystic

don't mistake me for santero

just because I speaky Spanish

no meano mio wear sombrero

I can be your cuz, homeboy, dude or bro

if you think my hair looks kinky

you're not looking at my curls

just a young fuckboy with a messy natural perm

am I Persian, am I Muslim, or Mexican —

on whose terms are we targeting?

It seems to change with every president

demilitarize our democracy

Cops are bad if they stand

for the broken system that we've had

I don't want to age to see this country

run into the stomping ground, show some urgency

fuck, give it back to the natives, it's sad to show

the depths of disparity we're not willing to let go

I still believe, I'll take arms for peace and love —

show me that America's still worth dreaming of.

A Better Word for Lightning

I break my constant vigil on this blank page
praying i can break whatever dam is in me
and let the words flow before my 11:59 deadline.
A thousand tiny particulates of frustration swarm
from out my frown with an exhale — were my vocal chords a
wind chime,
they would groan in the wind.

"This might sound weird, but there needs to be
a better word for lightning."

"I agree," my friend says, not looking away from his computer.

"You have fulmination, and that's a mouthful.
A bolt of lightning is even worse, and then there's
electrical discharge, and now
we're just bringing science into this.
There just needs to be a shorter and cleaner word, lightning
doesn't look like what it represents nor does it sound
like it means the violent, dramatic flash in the sky —
it's spelled like 'oh look a light turned on, light is happening,'
and that's a lot less impressive than this tree that sprawls out
in a fiery stream of plasma at 270,000 miles a second
it can reach the moon in 55 minutes,
there should be a word that

properly embodies that raw power bordering the
supernatural."

"Settle down," he laughs it off. "Ok,
so you have thunder, thunder goes boom.
Lightning is like a whish, a crackle, a kizapple."
"But those are not satisfying," I whine.
"Some words just aren't, it's
how you use them. Life
isn't satisfying, sometimes it just is.
Lightning just is."

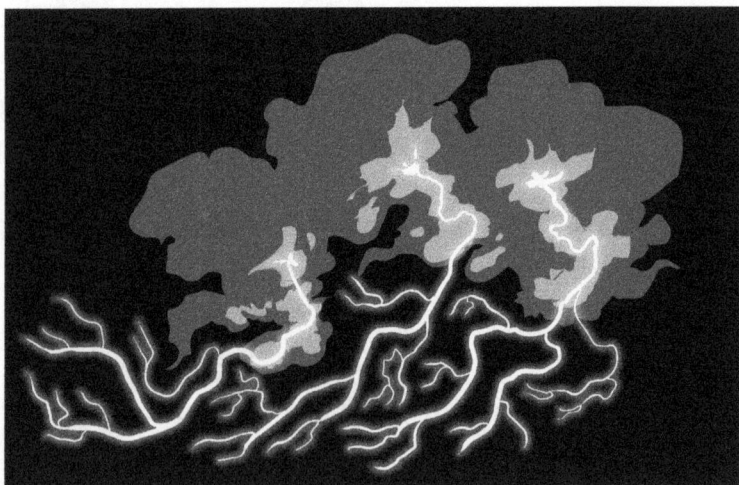

Agoraphobia

you're going to be okay

the room is not shrinking, it's in your head

throat dry, tightening by the second

no you don't have to panic

it's not that serious

I mean, I understand what you're going through

tunnel vision cuts off the reception

and forms a neat vignette in your field of view

and I say that not to dismiss you

not trying to diminish or cap

just relax your hands

remember to breathe

sitting in a roomful of strangers,

make a note in your memos for that memento mori

you'll get through it, you'll be home soon

just breathe

Affirmations in Liminal Spaces

I live in a house — but not a home.
I am a visitor — a guest star on crossover episodes
that usher in the newest season at my mother's home.
I got Steve'd when I went off to college — five hundred miles
away, my family tunes in.
I have transcontinental friendships — a sea of solid earth
between us.
I miss people I don't want to be around.
I miss faces I'm not around enough.

I will be thirty sooner than I'd want to be.
I am no teenage spirit nor am I adulting on my own.
I tally-mark question marks and quarter-life crises
— Mami sometimes ruminates of wild-haired grandchildren
while I'm here single like the last Pringle in the can
trying to get my shit together.
Only thing getting laid is my bed and
you can't even check my Facebook status.
I don't want to be a hoarder,
I want to be a memory dispenser.
I don't want gum or candy melted in the cupholders.
I don't want my children — or my grandchildren — to forget
my birthday.
I don't want polaroids bleached by exposure and suburban
neglect.

I want those faces hammered and nailed on fixtures of love —

a digital tapestry of our family history hanging on our walls.
I want my hugs and thank yous, my hellos and goodbyes
to be my signatures for the impressions I've left behind.

I live in a house — but not a home.
I was a homebody — I'm now a somebody.
I empty my closet and disembowel clothes from luggage
and either have too many hangers — or never enough.
I throw out old shirts, socks with peaky toes,
I keep my ripped jeans, my faded band tees,
nicotine is my ball I don't kick.
I have nerves of steel wool pads —
against dish and skin is the scratch and the itch.

I lived in a house — but not a home.
I miss hands I don't want to hold.
I light a candle for no one — just light up my phone screen.
I was a house — I strive to be
a face to call home for the future you and me.

American Graffiti

American graffiti
high rises eclipse all and everything
urban cartouches and neon hieroglyphs
like highway exits for the eye to u-turn
and take the long way downtown
the Walls a bleached coral white
to the heights of degradation
a nation stamped and slapped on
taped down and tagged on
riddled with slander and libel and quotes from the Bible
cirque du politique, a pop-up boutique
summer mixes popping off on the speakers
and tweakers on the streets, meager dirty and meek
watching traffic jam up, thin out and get heavier again
thunder under bridges, stampeding on the ramps
the bass and 808s kick harder than the bends
tear up rubber on the asphalt with trap house vibes
the rest is subsidized, the sun hitting their eyes
in hot pursuit for loftier and guccier things
supreme without the love, sitting in a cold train
dreampop clouds and hip hop of the soul
a lil bougie with a boogie dripped out in Brickell gold
link up with your Cuban friends
bodies wrapped in big brands
big cheese, rat race, fat cats, hedge maze

ace but not spayed, shovel with no face
you choose to flush dreams,
don't make it live on the stream
what you catch is what you keep
less you rolling in the deep

are you a trend chaser
or something outpacing ya
mumble cuz words ain't important
the feeling's captured in the moment
a single stolen frame, backshot to the brain
when you return to the sound
or the smell's plus one makes you fuckin break down
cuz it's been so long since you've been here
control you in the now
and work your way up, buttercup
sorries are hella safer than dealing with introspection
adulting isn't bolting at the first sign of friction
it's owning up to fuckups and fuckdowns, nonfiction
don't live life in superlatives, count your relatives
your six degrees, even if you go to college
that's not time wasted, it shows that you faced it
academic adversity, hard knocks, are you who's knocking
shit down stumbling after hours like "what's poppin"
what does it all mean to you, where you goin
what you doin, who you're doin it with
space race for the stars and moon with aim assist

persist, if you can't, cease and desist

come on, buttercup
you're too high up and you're motion sick
the buildup's a drop, lil butimstillakid
come back to earth, show up to class
and after just lay in the grass for a while
you've got no mileage, no isle is
a man that has yet to drown
settle down, lay down a settlement
the basis of your race is how you stay relevant
how you develop it, make room for the elephant
go all in zero fucks for the hell of it
you let it define you or let others fill your entry or
workshop the narrative enough for the pageantry
skin deep is where you leave off with the pleasantries
so what does that make for the rest of you
Is the best of you a testament
or are you forever a tenant in the body your were born in

—*Julia Fatou*—

Don't take more than you need

cause I'm not waiting for you

your mind was set the first time we fell out of touch

and go and touch and go

and touch

We are

complements to the other's set

but our axes pole shift, rip apart

cascade, entropy by design — it's an art

how we kid ourselves we'll

do better than the first time

how much more I iterate why

the sky's worth the wait

after the coming rain

Dust to laces

a million seahorse tails splintering into trees

embroider me

How much more do you have

to remind me of all the things we used to do

so much more than sleep in tiny beds

far too tired to peel off work clothes

my mouth is moving and there's nothing left to say

What do we do now?

The world's on fire

the hottest winds knock us down

Keanu Joaquin Del Toro

Rapping as Requested to a Total Stranger on a Dating Site (193 Days of Quarantine)

So by the looks of it,

By the books you fit

To have a good time if it's with the right kind

Of people misbehavin', the night is your haven

Where the music and the mood

come together when you're ravin'

Yeah, city lights and sounds taste better after rounds

Of screwdrivers and that bass that can make your chest pound

But I've been there, done that

getting wasted's old hat

I'm looking for the girl that's right for me

A little bookworm, my own Velma Dinkley

And I'd like to know a hint of your flow

And whiff your personality and learn what exact-a-ly

Brought you on here, where you're coming from

And whether or not you are a natural phenomenon

Is it more of pride or is there some prejudice?

Does wrath come from grapes or they just decorative, for emphasis?

Are you a glutton for food or pain or is there some evidence

That earthly pleasures leave no trace on your edifice?

Are you full of lust, or envious of any of us?

What kind of breed is the make of your greed

When you're behind the whip are you always top speed?

Not a sloth, but a koala? I'll be the eucalyptus

Just wanna know the lives and cities you've lived in

I wanna know the make of your soul, Secondqueen

Is it old, is it new, or somewhere in between?

Why aren't you first? That's where I'd place you-ou

Given the time to better learn you, for true-ue

Text me, call me, beep me

if you wanna reach me

Nothing's Kim Possible if you're Ron Stoppable

Tap away, give a like, hit reply, press send

Or whatever works better for you on your end

L8r, sk8r

Keanu Joaquin Del Toro

To Those of Us Who Are Concerned

To those of us who were once in a secret's leap of each other,
and folded our confidence in the notes we borrowed,

> I still remember your handwriting.

To those of us who would spontaneously combust into song to
embarrass each other,

> whose songs do you sing now?

To those of us who wrinkled the page for later because those
moments were just too good, with those years now yellow
with age,

> is it boxed up with other books in your closet or under
> your bed — or did you give it away instead?

To those of us who told each other that this stretch of grass
between lunch and gym was every city we could ever visit
when we finally get out of this school,

> are you still in town?

To those of who claimed that we'd all grow old together and
how our children would be best friends with each other,

> whose kids are you waiting for now?

To those of us who built forts out of ghost stories, plastic trays,
milk cartons, and euphoria bred from missing hallway passes,

> do any of our stories get told today?

To those of us who would squint at our canvases to find the values in our work,

> do you still squint in the mirror?

To those of us who claimed victory for surviving the flood and venturing beyond the teenage wasteland,

> what else do you have to bring to the table?

To those of us who don't go out anymore,

> how long has it been?

To those of us who are just another gum stain, lost in the trample of tardies, unrequited looks, and unenthused teenage iridescence,

> why did you never say you felt that way?

To those of us who are concerned,

> if you haven't been, don't be.

ADRIFT

haven't posted in a
while. #finalsweek
36 min. ago

— *MARIANA* —

The deepest depressions on earth are Mariana's

and the valleys carved in you

What We Leave Behind

I.   Antediluvian

I could start, and then you follow.

        I'm not sure about this. It's getting late —

It*'s already late,* she says.
I mean, we don't have to do this,
but if you want to...

Her eyes leap with the headlights that smear across weeping
windows. She sinks into her seat,
her outline along the shadow inside the car,
her late-night retreat. His voice
swims laps around her face,
her promontory,
racing against the tide that gushes and roars
with yeses and mores.
He trembles,
leans in — she unbuttons his shirt,
rolling back to bare his chest
for her hands and blonde head to follow his thin frame.
He goes for her bra, they shake off their shoes,
and press their chests against
each other, her heart arrhythmic
his strings unplayed.
They share the same breaths, tuning each chord
by rubbing palms against backs,

grasping and clutching joints and necks and wrists and hands.
His sloppy words against her ears,

Are you sure?

Yes, I'm ready.

She leans back, keeping a quiet gaze; she sinks
into the night trapped in this car, he watches
her, killing the sunlight still in his eyes. Their eyes hold
the quiet gaze with clasping hands, fingers woven
tight, palms pressed the way they want
them to. Her hands are
so cold. His are
so thin.
She opens
the door. He walks
in.

II.   Postdiluvian

She sets her luggage down for a moment
to get a better grip, he enters behind her
to turn on the lights — yellow hazy and uncertain.

The working bathroom's at the end of the hall,
straight down; can't miss it.

Thank you, she says,

and she follows the length of the apartment suite.

Hey,

she turns to him,

Are you sure you're ok?

Positive.

He takes the rest of her bags and she locks the bathroom
behind her
and looks at the mirror, her eyes still red, her fading blue hair
wet from rain;
she sits on the toilet, her hands won't stop shaking, and she
stares at her hands and feet.
Something is off about them, but she doesn't know what — she
reflects on how her
hands used to be thinner. Her breath is shaky,
and she clutches her hands together,
squeezing the air out between her palms,
squeezing her chest and her lungs and eyes
to feel something other than frustration, the stinging
from her tears and this cavity in her chest
waiting for the water to crash on down.
She flushes, watching the blue cleaner spiral and foam and
rush down the gullet of the pipe — her words do the same.

A sigh trembles out, and she wrings her hair over the sink. She
finds her bags in the bedroom,
sees her boyfriend snoring on his belly
and slips off her shoes and out of her pants and

sinks under the sheets — blue in blinded moonlight.
Her thoughts are islands across the ocean and dust tossed in
the breeze and paper home to scrawls
with fallen water left to freeze
and her feet — she knows what they're missing.

She bolts up and throws the blanket over her lover,
and she checks her shoes, unzips her bags, shakes her pants,
kneeling on the cold tile.

What's wrong, babe, what'd you lose? he asks in a low mumble.

I lost my ankle bracelet.

Her boyfriend breaths in and turns over,
folding the blanket into stiff ripples and waves,

The one you never take off?

*Yeah, I must've... I must've lost it somehow
at the house, or on the way here.*

D'you wanna get it back?

I... I dunno...

Well, he yawns, *just lemme know,*

and we'll go get it tomorrow.

But I don't know where it is.

We'll look for it tomorrow.

Ok...

As she reclines under the covers, the feeling sinks with her —
she's out on open waters — is she justified, or is she just
another hypocrite for running away?

Culturally-Inclusive Holiday Specials
on the Hallmark Channel

Last-minute Christmas lights flicker and twinkle on the wall,

the ones that change through five or so colors and have

different speed settings; the ones her mom always hated

because they were annoying to look at.

She sits on her boyfriend's couch with the big dip

that would leave her lopsided if she were sat

in the middle; they were eating Publix chicken,

mac n' cheese, mashed sweet potato (both microwavable),

and gingerbread Pop tarts while watching

culturally-inclusive holiday specials on the Hallmark channel.

She's snuggled up tight in a thick fuzzy blue

blanket while her boyfriend sits on the opposite end of her,

swiping across his phone screen.

She sniffles, and he looks up,

Babe, if you miss your folks, why don't we go see them?

I don't want to.

Are you sure?

I don't wanna see them, just drop it.

Ok...

She's not paying attention to the movie, it's pretty boring

anyway, and she checks her phone's home screen

— no new messages.

She sets her phone atop the table, and it chimes. She

takes it back up and it's a notification for Christmas sales

happening RIGHT NOW! HURRY BEFORE IT'S OVER!

She sighs, and tosses her phone to her side

as she undoes her blanket and gets up.

Oh, babe, can you bring some more
candy canes while you're up?

Sure, she says.

She enters the kitchen to pour herself a glass of water from

the tap, and plucks a candy cane from the

Christmas vines they hung up late last night.

She plops herself on the couch, and hands

her boyfriend the candy cane, and

sticks her hand down the cushion to retrieve her

phone. She goes into her messages;

the last one she sent was to her mom over two hours ago:

Merry Christmas!

Her eyes sting — she locks her phone

hugs her knees under the blanket.

Soon after, the credits roll as her

boyfriend says how lame it was.

She tosses the blanket off of her,

You can pick the next film if you want,

she mumbles.

Ok.

He goes to crouch by the TV to thumb through his personal

movie collection while she heads

for the bathroom in his room. Her phone

buzzes and lights up, a new message with a

photo attachment appears on her lock screen

— it's from her mom,

Merry Christmas! Love you, Jasmine.

Keanu Joaquin Del Toro

—ANTARCTICA—

he was crouching in the parking lot
ducking behind cars like a crackhead.
he was feeding into nicotine, meager frame,
the wind wasn't having it.
a mostly empty fishbowl sky, orange and pink
bleed into the evening blue, the burning smell
of frost hovering thousands of feet above.

she complained about her figure
solid flabs of muscle
body dysmorphic, self-loathing, autotrophic
why do i gravitate to girls like you?
pinned to the mist, foggy Friday sundown
a wraith wrapped in ripped jeans, oversized hoodies
coughing on the seat of his distress.

he pencils her in when something goes bump in his life
and she comes running every time
handfuls, heartfuls of cookies, brownies
leftover mac and cheese, tender understandings.
she's not quite sure how she got here
falling in and out of lust.

his body counts are high
but that never bothered her
what did was when they went unprotected.

so she wonders what she could've done different
while they were heavy on each other
packing heat into the corners of their bodies.
there are no condoms for the soul
no pills for love control. she had no plans
to foster heartbreak after heartbreak
she simply did, that's what other girls seemed to do.

her voice circling, flushing down his ear
the remnant of him still stuck on her lips
but that tingling was an outbreak.

something that she couldn't shake off was
how, why
why
why
why
when he was inside her
did he bring up her ex?
it always went back to her
and she never understood why
this beautiful boy has the past up for lease
and though they were the ones living together
she was living rent free.

jaz has been limp, flaccid
no chemical reaction for this acid in her mouth
her libido dropped faster than albedo at the poles.

splash of midnight faucet water, nerves
crackle and spark and glow, ringlets of red hair,
miles of her simply want to untangle, see how far she
can stretch, cables cross the ocean floor.
sunken, hidden, routinely ridden in an unmade bed
like a wild, green Antarctica,
whose hips and breasts haven't seen sunlight in millenia,
buried under mountains of snow and desolation.
a part of her can break off, travel down the drain,
or evaporate, hitch a ride with a cloud,
find a colder place to be, somewhere
the heat of the night can't reach her. but
the tide pulls her in, coriolis, planetary spin
rock her to warmer waters, she will melt,
reincarnate into a hurricane, a heat wave,
she is co2, she is the crisis.

drowning in the saltwater mixing with the fresh
all the life in her, at the end of a drag,
coming to a slow boil.

Wearing Pants Unisexually

I see horse riders pummeling the pontic

chasing wind and sun

a skyful of clouds

swimming, soaring in herds.

amazons, they wore pants —

figures black and red

with enough attention

enough appreciation

dim in their shine

thousands of years after

show these women wearing pants

to prevent chafing on horseback

on ridgeback

on steppeback

forth and onward into nebulous seas of green

the dala, the prairie of asia major.

in my late holocene

the taíno in me remembers the warm

smell of caribbean waters,

the zapotec in me tastes the sweet and salt

on my peach-fuzz lip.

the ethiopian highlander, and lowlander, too,

each cling true to the inherent safety

in the boughs of trees.

the zygote I once was

helps me breed new blood

the iron in my bones

tangled in my chromosomes

looks to the sky, reflecting back

on its swaddle, cradled in

the womb of the star

that went supernova

— the afterbirth

of a million

trillion

births.

so yeah —

I'll wear the pants in this relationship

not to dominate or tame you

but because they're sensible

to prevent chafing,

because they're comfortable.

I wear the pants

you don't want to.

Ephemeral Earthenware

Flexible then stern,
s'it image or imago
waiting for the kiln?

Cartographers of Human Nature

Your face with its natural geography

with laughter that raises smiling cheeks

forming horizons that block out the lamp over your desk

I don't want this moment to go to waste

we were just cuddling and giggling whispers

in the hot and heavy darkness a moment ago

and I just had to hold more than this gaze

I held the air, the sheets, the bed,

the apologies for saying sorry so much

the thing about low pressure is that thunder still rolls in

thought bubbles clap over us, and at some point

I had to let myself breathe it all out

I didn't catch feelings

I went looking for them

I hunted them, skinned them,

prepared a meal from them

and fed it to you

then all the *if onlys* start pouring in

—1851—

we sat there

watching the squirrels rustle and skitter overhead,

wooden hands spread mossy flaky fingers latticed

above — the glint of twilight in our eyes —

caffeine and the comedown we sprawled out
on the green, world weary, two weeks left of class —
i said,

>   "you may think otherwise, and your insecurities and…
>   everything else may, too… but you're one of the
>   greatest things this world has to offer."

in reply,

>   "why? why did you say that?"

>   "because it's true, because you exist… and i met you."

>   "… i met you, too."

and you giggle and smile and laugh in a way that is so you
it's this face
this face you've left in the closet
in a shoebox full of two-year-old photographs
that have sat from a year
and beyond
and i'm honored to see you smile that way
because i said something, i did something —

i always want what i shouldn't have

i can live life with another sister

you can be that for me instead
it never needed to be brought up
but i'm sure there were signs that showed otherwise and
you study anthropology, you know how humans work
but i should find some soil to make peace with that feeling
all i should do is sift through the dirt, tend to the soil

we could gaze the stars or go to space together
electric sheep grazing the cosmos instead of sleep
i want to swallow your mango mist
your favorite song this week tastes like pineapple
and your favorite genre of country music
is the one where the Native Americans were right
and you're a moon, a wink and you're gone, yet
you are comet incarnate across the surface of my eye
you're on a whole other orbit full of different skylines
despite the radio in our deep space buzzing together
you are the summer heat and its soothing breeze
mediterranean whispers from the shouts
of a thousand generations of italian mothers and men
a part of you fades in and out of days, out of years
the cascading jazz of bygone decades and childish wonder
that you reawaken in me
but because all i wanna do is hold you —

if i were too close for comfort —
because i loved your best friend before

i really got to know you —
your restless heart will look for skies that match your hair
that eerie green where the algae meets by the shore
and those deep seated blues that never escape you

i know that these next few months
will show which way our leaves will blow
and i will still keep reading them
and be mindful and sorry
that summer will keep you busy and fun
without me
cause there's a boy from home that's counting down the days
and while you retreat to that familiar south
i'll brave the waters lapping the great white north
and we'll be just a few winks away
and bring each other back with all our strangers made friends
until more of our own leaves shudder, gather, and fall
and maybe
just maybe
this beautiful life won't cut us down after all
then i'll be able to fill a shoebox of my own

WASTELAND

(GEOGLYPH)

Levis spoke of places

where the eye starves,

Murillo where the ear

learns famine, and

in these moments, along these landmarks

where songlines are the only way through,

her mouth knows drought. her fingers

snap in the cold, tinged in the stink

of smoke she bummed off. hot and sad

all summer, habitual bummer

in a band of lonely hearts;

angsty in her autumn,

brooding in royal jealousy.

swept along the waist,

hives droning, rising,

taking their time,

as hills and mountains do,

to collapse, heave and brush and stroke

and lacquer together a wind-washed plateau.

hands twinge, between leverage, thumb's mesa

and balance of forefinger, she forgets how to write

gs and zs and qs in her cursive-print hybrid, unorthodox

ligatures ligaments to her absentmindedness, losing

herself between the lines and beyond the margins

where few dare	to go. how, what,
who is she if	she does not know
where she begins	where she ends?
a finger tracing	stretchmarks along her
thighs remind her	of naked riverbeds,
they still remember	the shape of water.

In My Late Holocene (An Open Letter to You)

My ancestors survived not just one,
but every ice age, the Last Glacial Maximum
twenty thousand years ago, when ice covered
more than ten percent of the planet, land and sea, when
most of the terrain along the 45th and 40th degrees
parallel were tundra and taiga. Mammoths, mastodons,
sabertooths, giant sloths, monsters real and imagined,
my ancestors drove them all to annihilation,
and so we entered the sixth mass extinction event.
There are no Ticketmaster prices for it, you are the ticket,
you are the master. Global warming but one price we pay.
My ancestors suffered the second
death over and over and over.
I will never know all their names.
My ancestors planted the first seeds that fed a tribe that
coalesced into a nation, my ancestors survived mythology,
prehistory, wove into the fabrics and textiles of society.
They survived Toba, Neanderthals, volcanic winters,
my ancestors sailed across the Atlantic
and passed through Beringia. My ancestors
survived plague, chickenpox, smallpox, malaria,
yellow fever, leprosy, depression, famine, drought,
war and conquest, inquisition, persecution, slavery, genocide,
desecration, deforestation, and sea level rise.
Funny enough, yours likely did, too.

These were the prices they paid in full.
Our ancestors spread out from Africa, grew feet from hands,
lost their tails, broke and chipped teeth and bones and
rock and stone to fashion tools and weapons.
Our magic system IRL is simply
delicately and carefully putting things
together in the exact way they need to in order for
them to do what we want, from shoelaces with a
loopty loop and pull to airplanes and smartphones. In every
single change and phase and turn and season,
the tree of life endured, and we are the fruit of
all that hardship, the largest scale model of trial
and error imaginable.

Don't waste it.

Without your ancestors going through all of that shit,
you would not be here. Without the cooperation
and exploitation back then and happening right now
every day, you would not know luxury the way
the algorithm feeds it to you. We can be better.
We have done it before.
Be grateful for life's lovely mistakes, own your failures,
give thanks for hitching a ride on the little blue dot
during a time when we have Netflix and Youtube and
vegan cookie dough ice cream and video games and memes.

Help others, especially when they need it. Help yourself,
because you will always need it. Give hugs
often, say *I love you* more, slowly weed *hate* out
of your vocabulary. Take a DNA test. Walk your dogs, clean
the litter box, put away the rumpled clothes on your
chair or on the corner of your bed. As you sit under
the canopy of your family tree, remember
where you come from. Enjoy what
others don't, enjoy the breeze, it ain't
gonna last long for you or me.

Her Arms Were Oceans Wide

"Too much sank into my depths,
too long did I lie in wait — I sat so long
barnacles made flesh of me."

Palms and banyans and mangroves
trade seed and words with the breeze.
Only recently has she made pilgrimage
surviving the bends. Troves resurfaced,
most of it a quaint memory or two, but
she remembers, she no longer shrouds them
beneath the twilight. Self sabotaging,
turbulent — the coral was her brain, she bleached it.

She beached her whales.

Jasmine circumnavigated and constellated
some greater, wider somewhere
and the allnighters were close enough.

"Let me bask in my glory, in my contact high
for even being alive. Let the foam
carry me back to shore,
the tire tube do the work."

When you've got nothing left to say
as it comes, let the quiet sit in your mouth, on
your crown, your brow, welcome it
to your ear, lean it on your shoulder.
Lay it on your lap. Should it be salty, bitter, unripe,
that means it needs more time.

On the liminal and the littoral, on confluence
of salt, sand and sky, her arms were oceans wide
and beyond the horizon, the stars take a dip,
and as sure as they climb with every moonrise,
together, they are alive. In a year, she has lived
ten lifetimes, worn a thousand faces; she
will be a thousand more. At one point or another
her fingernails, her damaged hair
were the colors of
every hue and shade the
human eye could see.

She does not have it all figured out.

She is flawed. Very flawed.

She accepts herself to be.

Listen to the songs that played on loop
through the writing process

The Eve of Our Generation

Notes & Acknowledgements

You made it to the end of the book, congratulations! I had a handful of these poems scattered across two phones, lost in composition notebooks, and even on receipt papers for a while before I typed them up, and with a little fire under my ass, I was able to decipher and transcribe them. The oldest poem to my recollection is *To Those of Us Who Are Concerned*, written around 2018 — I've been an angsty little fuck for a long stretch of my life. A handful were written between then and throughout college, about half came out of quarantine with me, and the rest were written during the production of this book.

When the lockdown began, I was a senior in university, and I told myself that I would finally take my writing seriously, so I used all of that free time to write poems, short stories, that one novel that never seems to end, watched Death Note for the first time (anime and movie), and gained 35 lbs.

I have quite a few references to media I've consumed, nods to authors I appreciate, and other random little things that are (mostly) Google-able, so I'll throw you a bone to get you started:

The name "Julia Fatou" comes from two mathematicians, Gaston Julia and Pierre Fatou, who were instrumental in the understanding behind fractals and giving them a function, popularized and elaborated by Benoit B. Mandelbrot in the 1970s. How pretentious is that? I also recommend you google

"Julia set" and "Douady rabbit" to see some trippy fractals, and take a light read on some chaos theory if you have the chance (this will be on the final). There are so many more little secrets here and there, the rest is up to you.

Jasmine's story is part of a larger narrative that will one day be given even more life and depth than the glimpses seen here. At first, I didn't know how to include her poems, but I wrote everything out until I realized that to do her justice, she needed to be the majority of the book. There's so much that I haven't even delved into, but we'll just save all that for another day.

In my early tweens, I was writing song lyrics that would never be finished, I was too self-conscious to share them. I then had a galaxy brain moment — some of my favorite songs could be read as poems, and some songs were originally poems, and that convinced me that there was more going on with poetry than I originally gave it credit for. It was one of those things that you can't unsee once you see it, so I pumped out terrible poem after poem, consuming Edgar Allen Poe, reading my mandatory Billy Shaking-His-Speare, Emily Dickinson, Ralph Waldo Emerson, and other dead people. I really enjoyed English class (wow, what a shocker). It wasn't until my late teens that I read more contemporary poetry; I recommend you grab a copy of John Murillo's *Up Jump the Boogie* and Eve L. Ewing's *Electric Arches* and anything by Ocean Vuong. They left pretty big impressions on me.

I would like to thank my mother, Wajima, who not only raised a very handsome young man, but would also have me read the dictionary when I was on time out as a kid. I hated it so much I learned to enjoy it, and I now have an English degree and a million Wikipedia bookmarks, all thanks to treating dictionary entries as a personal snack. *Mami, you taught me to be the man I needed growing up and the man I need to be now, and I am grateful everyday for your love, your patience and your wit.*

Chris, thank you for creating the cover of this book, for being a beautiful bastard and my lifelong friend, my brother from another mother.

Jei, my right-hand man, my battle buddy, my brother from the same mother, who I have shared my worries, my dreams, my music with, and who I habitually watch cringey and worthwhile films and tv with, thank you for being you.

Kassy, my little big sister, you deserve everything good in this world and you eventually get it.

Buba, papo, you deserve everything good in this world and you eventually break it.

Antonio, thank you for being the best roommate we could ask for. Our home has been joyous and colorful in an otherwise bleak and tragic year, and you have contributed so much to that since you came into our lives.

Donna Troy the French Boxer, Zeus the Shih Tzu, O-Ren Ishii the Wolf, Elsa and her kittens, Artemis, Joe and Kamala, thank you for being my emotional support animals, please stop peeing on my bed.

I would also like to thank my publisher and editor, Flor Ana Mireles. I am beyond grateful for working with you over the last six months on this book and for the heart and care you've put into it. You are a talented writer and I look forward with great earnest to your ever-growing bibliography.

Dalton, Sequoia and Ravza, thank you for putting up with my rants and my friendship, my professors for putting up with my tardiness, and all others that have touched my heart and stimulated my mind along the way.

And last, but not least, thank *you* (yes, you) for being a part of my journey. You have read a lot of personal stuff; gossip accordingly.

About The Author

Keanu Joaquin Del Toro is an Latino-American writer who made his literary debut with his short story _The Lionfish Flower_ in the anthology _Stories From The Forest_. Hailing from the Sunshine State, Keanu wrote for his school paper _The FSView & Florida Flambeau_, and graduated with a BA in Creative Writing and a Minor in Film Studies. His stories often focus on the misadventures of angsty teens and twenty-somethings while his poetry focuses on the little things as well as the big things in life: love, depression, tequeños, paradise lost and found, and more. Keanu began writing from a young age, has a lifelong love for poetry, and even had a phase in his mid-teens where he convinced himself he didn't like poems even though he always went back to them; he's glad that was short-lived. _The Eve of Our Generation_ was originally a sporadic series of poems that were outlets for his anxiety and goofy demeanor, which evolved into an exercise in ~~futility~~ storytelling, where he explores different perspectives and conflicted feelings through verse.